OUR
Family
TREE
AND
ALBUM

The Five Mile Press Pty Ltd
415 Jackson St, San Francisco
CA, 94111, USA
Email: publishing@fivemile.com.au
Website: www.fivemile.com.au

First published 2002
This revised edition first published 2008

Reprinted 2008

Edited by Samone Bos
Designed by SBR Productions, Olinda, Victoria
Printed in China

ISBN 978 1 74124 614 8

Please note: all internet addresses were correct at the
time this book was printed. However, due to the dynamic nature
of the internet, these addresses may change over time.

Contents

Introduction

Here in the United States of America, our population of over three hundred million supports a varied richness of cultures and peoples. And every one of us has a story to tell. It could be that your ancestors were plantation owners or sought their luck as gold prospectors. Perhaps they traveled great distances to be where you now call home, lured to foreign shores with the dream of starting a new life. They may have been one of the twelve million people to pass through Ellis Island. And maybe there was a heart-wrenching separation between loved ones during war or times of hardship. Share the story of your ancestry with your own family in this beautiful book specially designed for your precious memories.

Our Family Tree and Album is a means of chronicling and reflecting upon those very special people who make up your family and the history that you share. By compiling a family tree and album, you are bestowing upon future generations a marvelous and irreplaceable gift – an intimate insight into the people who made their own existence possible.

Contacts

Building a family tree can be a long and arduous journey. Sometimes, there may be gaps that you cannot fill without the assistance of professional organizations. Further guidance on how to construct your family tree can be obtained from genealogical and historical societies such as the following:

The National Archives and Records Administration
8601 Adelphi Road
College Park, MD 20740-6001

www.archives.gov/genealogy

US State Archives

www.archives.gov/research/alic/reference/state-archives.html

National Association of Government Archives and Records Administrators
Suite 1009, 90 State Street
Albany, New York 12207

www.nagara.org/index.cfm

Federation of Genealogical Societies
PO Box 200940
Austin, TX 78720-0940

www.fgs.org/index.php

Immigration History Research Center – University of Minnesota
Elmer L Andersen Library,
Suite 311, 222 21st Ave S
Minneapolis MN 55455

www.ihrc.umn.edu

The Library of Congress – Local History and Genealogy Reading Room
101 Independence Ave SE,
Thomas Jefferson Building, LJ G42
Washington, DC 20540-4660

www.loc.gov/rr/genealogy

National Society of Daughters of the American Revolution
1776 D Street, NW
Washington, DC 20006-5303

www.dar.org/library/speccol.cfm

Genealogy.com
Offers tips on starting genealogical research, web links, and a 470-million-name searchable database.

www.genealogy.com

The Internet Public Library
Links to genealogy research tools, guidance, and websites.
www.ipl.org/div/subject/browse/ref40.00.00

I can trace my ancestry back to a protoplasmal primordial atomic globule.
W.S. GILBERT, THE MIKADO

About Our Family

MOTHER'S FULL NAME	**FATHER'S FULL NAME**
NICKNAME(S)	NICKNAME(S)
SIGNATURE	SIGNATURE
DATE AND TIME OF BIRTH	DATE AND TIME OF BIRTH
BIRTHPLACE	BIRTHPLACE
STAR SIGN	STAR SIGN
OCCUPATION	OCCUPATION
HOBBIES/PASTIMES	HOBBIES/PASTIMES
FAVORITE COLOR	FAVORITE COLOR
FAVORITE SONG	FAVORITE SONG
FAVORITE BOOK	FAVORITE BOOK
FAVORITE FILM/TELEVISION SHOW	FAVORITE FILM/TELEVISION SHOW
FAVORITE FOOD	FAVORITE FOOD
CHILDHOOD IDOLS/HEROES	CHILDHOOD IDOLS/HEROES
HAPPIEST MOMENT	HAPPIEST MOMENT
SADDEST MOMENT	SADDEST MOMENT
DATE	*DATE*

FIRST CHILD'S FULL NAME

NICKNAME(S)

SIGNATURE

DATE AND TIME OF BIRTH

BIRTHPLACE

STAR SIGN

OCCUPATION

HOBBIES/PASTIMES

FAVORITE COLOR

FAVORITE SONG

FAVORITE BOOK

FAVORITE FILM/TELEVISION SHOW

FAVORITE FOOD

CHILDHOOD IDOLS/HEROES

HAPPIEST MOMENT

SADDEST MOMENT

DATE

SECOND CHILD'S FULL NAME

NICKNAME(S)

SIGNATURE

DATE AND TIME OF BIRTH

BIRTHPLACE

STAR SIGN

OCCUPATION

HOBBIES/PASTIMES

FAVORITE COLOR

FAVORITE SONG

FAVORITE BOOK

FAVORITE FILM/TELEVISION SHOW

FAVORITE FOOD

CHILDHOOD IDOLS/HEROES

HAPPIEST MOMENT

SADDEST MOMENT

DATE

Third Child's full name	**Fourth Child's full name**
Nickname(s)	Nickname(s)
Signature	Signature
Date and time of birth	Date and time of birth
Birthplace	Birthplace
Star sign	Star sign
Occupation	Occupation
Hobbies/pastimes	Hobbies/pastimes
Favorite color	Favorite color
Favorite song	Favorite song
Favorite book	Favorite book
Favorite film/television show	Favorite film/television show
Favorite food	Favorite food
Childhood idols/heroes	Childhood idols/heroes
Happiest moment	Happiest moment
Saddest moment	Saddest moment
Date	*Date*

Photographs

There is scarcely any less trouble in running a family than in governing an entire state.
MICHEL DE MONTAIGNE

Our Family Tree

WIFE'S FULL NAME

HUSBAND'S FULL NAME

DATE OF MARRIAGE

PLACE OF MARRIAGE

CHILDREN

WIFE'S FATHER'S FULL NAME
_____

WIFE'S MOTHER'S FULL NAME
_____

DATE OF MARRIAGE
_____

PLACE OF MARRIAGE
_____

CHILDREN
_____
_____
_____

HUSBAND'S FATHER'S FULL NAME
_____

HUSBAND'S MOTHER'S FULL NAME
_____

DATE OF MARRIAGE
_____

PLACE OF MARRIAGE
_____

CHILDREN
_____
_____
_____

WIFE'S PATERNAL GRANDFATHER'S FULL NAME
_____

WIFE'S PATERNAL GRANDMOTHER'S FULL NAME
_____

DATE OF MARRIAGE
_____

PLACE OF MARRIAGE
_____

CHILDREN
_____
_____

WIFE'S MATERNAL GRANDFATHER'S FULL NAME
_____

WIFE'S MATERNAL GRANDMOTHER'S FULL NAME
_____

DATE OF MARRIAGE
_____

PLACE OF MARRIAGE
_____

CHILDREN
_____
_____

HUSBAND'S PATERNAL GRANDFATHER'S FULL NAME
_____

HUSBAND'S PATERNAL GRANDMOTHER'S FULL NAME
_____

DATE OF MARRIAGE
_____

PLACE OF MARRIAGE
_____

CHILDREN
_____
_____

HUSBAND'S MATERNAL GRANDFATHER'S FULL NAME
_____

HUSBAND'S MATERNAL GRANDMOTHER'S FULL NAME
_____

DATE OF MARRIAGE
_____

PLACE OF MARRIAGE
_____

CHILDREN
_____
_____

WIFE'S GREAT-GRANDFATHER'S FULL NAME (PATERNAL GRANDFATHER'S FATHER)

WIFE'S GREAT-GRANDMOTHER'S FULL NAME (PATERNAL GRANDFATHER'S MOTHER)

DATE OF MARRIAGE

PLACE OF MARRIAGE

CHILDREN

WIFE'S GREAT-GRANDFATHER'S FULL NAME (PATERNAL GRANDMOTHER'S FATHER)

WIFE'S GREAT-GRANDMOTHER'S FULL NAME (PATERNAL GRANDMOTHER'S MOTHER)

DATE OF MARRIAGE

PLACE OF MARRIAGE

CHILDREN

WIFE'S GREAT-GRANDFATHER'S FULL NAME (MATERNAL GRANDFATHER'S FATHER)

WIFE'S GREAT-GRANDMOTHER'S FULL NAME (MATERNAL GRANDFATHER'S MOTHER)

DATE OF MARRIAGE

PLACE OF MARRIAGE

CHILDREN

WIFE'S GREAT-GRANDFATHER'S FULL NAME (MATERNAL GRANDMOTHER'S FATHER)

WIFE'S GREAT-GRANDMOTHER'S FULL NAME (MATERNAL GRANDMOTHER'S MOTHER)

DATE OF MARRIAGE

PLACE OF MARRIAGE

CHILDREN

HUSBAND'S GREAT-GRANDFATHER'S FULL NAME (PATERNAL GRANDFATHER'S FATHER)

HUSBAND'S GREAT-GRANDMOTHER'S FULL NAME (PATERNAL GRANDFATHER'S MOTHER)

DATE OF MARRIAGE

PLACE OF MARRIAGE

CHILDREN

HUSBAND'S GREAT-GRANDFATHER'S FULL NAME (PATERNAL GRANDMOTHER'S FATHER)

HUSBAND'S GREAT-GRANDMOTHER'S FULL NAME (PATERNAL GRANDMOTHER'S MOTHER)

DATE OF MARRIAGE

PLACE OF MARRIAGE

CHILDREN

HUSBAND'S GREAT-GRANDFATHER'S FULL NAME (MATERNAL GRANDFATHER'S FATHER)

HUSBAND'S GREAT-GRANDMOTHER'S FULL NAME (MATERNAL GRANDFATHER'S MOTHER)

DATE OF MARRIAGE

PLACE OF MARRIAGE

CHILDREN

HUSBAND'S GREAT-GRANDFATHER'S FULL NAME (MATERNAL GRANDMOTHER'S FATHER)

HUSBAND'S GREAT-GRANDMOTHER'S FULL NAME (MATERNAL GRANDMOTHER'S MOTHER)

DATE OF MARRIAGE

PLACE OF MARRIAGE

CHILDREN

A person may be indebted for a nose or an eye, for a graceful carriage or a voluble discourse, to a great-aunt or uncle, whose existence he has scarcely heard of.
WILLIAM HAZLITT

Mother's Family Tree

MOTHER'S MATERNAL GRANDMOTHER

DATE OF BIRTH

BIRTHPLACE

PARENTS

SIBLINGS

INTERESTS

MOTHER'S MATERNAL AUNTS AND UNCLES

MOTHER'S MATERNAL COUSINS

MOTHER'S MATERNAL GRANDFATHER

DATE OF BIRTH

BIRTHPLACE

PARENTS

SIBLINGS

INTERESTS

MOTHER'S MOTHER

DATE OF BIRTH

BIRTHPLACE

INTERESTS

(PHOTOGRAPH)

MOTHER

Mother's Family Tree

MOTHER'S PATERNAL GRANDMOTHER

_____

DATE OF BIRTH

_____

BIRTHPLACE

_____

PARENTS

_____

SIBLINGS

_____

INTERESTS

_____

_____

MOTHER'S FATHER

_____

DATE OF BIRTH

_____

BIRTHPLACE

_____

INTERESTS

_____

_____

MOTHER'S SIBLINGS   MOTHER'S BLOOD NIECES AND NEPHEWS

_____   _____

_____   _____

_____   _____

_____   _____

MOTHER'S PATERNAL GRANDFATHER

DATE OF BIRTH

BIRTHPLACE

PARENTS

SIBLINGS

INTERESTS

MOTHER'S PATERNAL AUNTS AND UNCLES

MOTHER'S PATERNAL COUSINS

A mother does not hear the music of the dance when her children cry.
GERMAN PROVERB

Mother's Childhood Memories

Long hot summers spent playing outdoors with friends or holidaying at the seaside with family are generic memories of an American childhood. Take yourself back to that wonder-filled time of when you were growing up.

WHAT ARE YOUR FIRST EVER MEMORIES?

HOW WERE THE HAPPIEST MOMENTS OF YOUR CHILDHOOD SPENT?

WHAT WERE YOUR FAVORITE GAMES OR SPORTS TO PLAY AS A CHILD?

WHAT WAS YOUR MOST TREASURED TOY OR STORYBOOK?

WHAT WAS YOUR NEIGHBORHOOD LIKE?

WHAT WAS YOUR FIRST PET?

WHAT WAS YOUR FAVORITE ANIMAL?

DID YOU HAVE A FAVORITE SIBLING, GRANDPARENT, AUNT, UNCLE, OR COUSIN?

WHAT MADE THEM SPECIAL TO YOU?

WHO WERE YOUR FIRST FRIENDS, AND HOW DID YOU MEET?

WHERE DID YOU ESPECIALLY LIKE TO VISIT AS A CHILD?

WHAT SORT OF THINGS MADE YOU LAUGH?

WERE THERE ANY SPECIAL GAMES THAT WERE UNIQUE TO YOUR FAMILY?

Photographs

The scenes of childhood are the memories of future years.

Father's Family Tree

FATHER'S MATERNAL GRANDMOTHER

DATE OF BIRTH

BIRTHPLACE

PARENTS

SIBLINGS

INTERESTS

FATHER'S MATERNAL AUNTS AND UNCLES

FATHER'S MATERNAL COUSINS

Father's maternal grandfather

Date of birth

Birthplace

Parents

Siblings

Interests

Father's mother

Date of birth

Birthplace

Interests

(PHOTOGRAPH)

Father

Father's Family Tree

FATHER'S PATERNAL GRANDMOTHER

DATE OF BIRTH

BIRTHPLACE

PARENTS

SIBLINGS

INTERESTS

FATHER'S FATHER

DATE OF BIRTH

BIRTHPLACE

INTERESTS

FATHER'S SIBLINGS   **FATHER'S BLOOD NIECES AND NEPHEWS**

FATHER'S PATERNAL GRANDFATHER

DATE OF BIRTH

BIRTHPLACE

PARENTS

SIBLINGS

INTERESTS

FATHER'S PATERNAL AUNTS AND UNCLES

FATHER'S PATERNAL COUSINS

How marvelous, wide and broad is my inheritance!
GOETHE

Father's Childhood Memories

Long hot summers spent playing outdoors with friends or holidaying at the seaside with family are generic memories of an American childhood. Take yourself back to that wonder-filled time of when you were growing up.

WHAT ARE YOUR FIRST EVER MEMORIES?

HOW WERE THE HAPPIEST MOMENTS OF YOUR CHILDHOOD SPENT?

WHAT WERE YOUR FAVORITE GAMES OR SPORTS TO PLAY AS A CHILD?

WHAT WAS YOUR MOST TREASURED TOY OR STORYBOOK?

WHAT WAS YOUR NEIGHBORHOOD LIKE?

WHAT WAS YOUR FIRST PET?

WHAT WAS YOUR FAVORITE ANIMAL?

DID YOU HAVE A FAVORITE SIBLING, GRANDPARENT, AUNT, UNCLE, OR COUSIN?

WHAT MADE THEM SPECIAL TO YOU?

WHO WERE YOUR FIRST FRIENDS, AND HOW DID YOU MEET?

WHERE DID YOU ESPECIALLY LIKE TO VISIT AS A CHILD?

WHAT SORT OF THINGS MADE YOU LAUGH?

WERE THERE ANY SPECIAL GAMES THAT WERE UNIQUE TO YOUR FAMILY?

Photographs

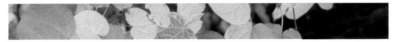

In youth we learn; in age we understand.
MARIE VON EBNER-ESCHENBACH

When We First Met

Hark back to the starry-eyed times of when love struck, fate flickered, and you stumbled across your future mate.
Did you meet at school, work, church, or a social gathering? Were you introduced through friends or family?
Perhaps there was a matchmaker in the midst!

HOW AND WHERE DID YOU FIRST MEET?

_____

_____

_____

WHAT WERE YOUR FIRST IMPRESSIONS OF ONE ANOTHER?

_____

_____

_____

DO YOU RECALL WHAT YOU WERE WEARING?

_____

_____

_____

HOW SOON AFTER MEETING WAS YOUR FIRST DATE, AND WHERE DID YOU GO?

_____

_____

_____

_____

How was your first date arranged?

_____

_____

_____

Do you recall how you felt on your first date, and the topics that were discussed?

_____

_____

_____

Share any other fond memories of when you met and the ensuing first date.

_____

_____

_____

Love laughs at locksmiths.
Proverb

Our Courtship

Offer your family a glimpse into the early days of your relationship, your courtship,
back when you were young, footloose, and fancy-free!

WHAT QUALITIES DID YOU FIRST FIND ATTRACTIVE IN ONE ANOTHER?

_____

_____

TO WHAT FEATS DID YOU TRY TO IMPRESS ONE ANOTHER? DID ONE PERSON ACTIVELY PURSUE THE OTHER TO
BEGIN WITH, OR WAS THE COURTSHIP OF EQUAL INTEREST?

_____

_____

WHERE DID YOU SPEND TIME TOGETHER? DID YOU HAVE A SPECIAL PLACE YOU LIKED TO VISIT?

_____

WHAT WAS THE FUNNIEST MOMENT IN YOUR EARLY DAYS TOGETHER?

_____

WHO WAS THE FIRST PERSON TO SAY 'I LOVE YOU', AND WHEN WAS IT SAID?

_____

WAS THERE A SPECIAL SONG YOU TERMED 'OUR SONG'? IF SO, HOW DID THIS SONG COME TO BE YOURS?

_____

SHARE ANY OTHER FOND MEMORIES YOU HAVE OF YOUR COURTSHIP.

_____

_____

_____

_____

Photographs

He who has daughters is always a shepherd.
OLD SAYING

Our Wedding Day

DATE AND TIME

PLACE OF CEREMONY

PRIEST/MINISTER/CELEBRANT

MATRON OF HONOR

BRIDESMAIDS

FLOWER GIRLS

BEST MAN

GROOMSMEN

PAGEBOYS

PLACE OF RECEPTION

NUMBER IN ATTENDANCE

Photographs

Our Wedding Day

WHAT WAS THE WEATHER LIKE ON YOUR WEDDING DAY?

HOW DID YOU BOTH FEEL BEFORE THE CEREMONY?

HOW DID THE BRIDE, GROOM, AND WEDDING PARTY ARRIVE?

WAS THERE ANY NOTABLE WORLD NEWS ON THE DAY (ASIDE FROM YOUR WEDDING, OF COURSE!)

WHAT FOOD WAS SERVED?

DESCRIBE YOUR WEDDING CAKE

WHAT SPECIAL SONGS WERE PLAYED AT YOUR WEDDING? TO WHICH SONG DID YOU DANCE YOUR WEDDING WALTZ?

WHO MADE THE WEDDING SPEECHES? CAN YOU RECALL ANY HUMOROUS OR PARTICULARLY TOUCHING THINGS THAT WERE SAID?

SHARE ANY OTHER FOND MEMORIES YOU HAVE OF YOUR WEDDING DAY.

Photographs

There is no more lovely, friendly, and charming relationship, communion, or company than a good marriage.
MARTIN LUTHER

Our Honeymoon

The deserved antidote to the flurry of the wedding day is the sweet relaxation of the honeymoon!
How did you choose to spend your first holiday as husband and wife?

_____

DESTINATION

_____

HOTEL/RESORT STAYED AT

_____

DURATION

Photographs

Our Honeymoon

SHARE THE FONDEST MEMORIES YOU HAVE OF YOUR HONEYMOON

_____

_____

_____

_____

_____

_____

_____

_____

_____

_____

_____

_____

_____

Photographs

Grow old along with me. The best is yet to be.
ROBERT BROWNING

Our Early Days

Alas, the early days of a marriage cannot be navigated through romantic bliss alone.
Certainly, it takes hard work to establish a life together as husband and wife.
What were your 'early days' like?

WHEN YOU CAME BACK FROM THE HONEYMOON WHERE DID YOU LIVE?

_____

_____

WHERE DID YOU BOTH WORK?

_____

_____

HOW DID YOU SPEND YOUR TIME TOGETHER IN THE EARLY DAYS OF YOUR MARRIAGE?
WERE THERE SPECIAL CLUBS, SPORTING EVENTS, OR RESTAURANTS THAT YOU FREQUENTED?

_____

_____

_____

WHAT WAS THE FIRST 'GOOD' DECOR ITEM/PIECE OF FURNITURE THAT YOU PURCHASED TOGETHER?

_____

HOW MANY CHILDREN DID YOU IMAGINE THAT YOU WOULD ONE DAY HAVE? HAD YOU DECIDED ON POTENTIAL NAMES FOR THESE CHILDREN?

_____

_____

_____

WHAT WAS THE FIRST PET YOU ADOPTED TOGETHER?

_____

Photographs

After the ecstasy, the laundry.
BUDDHIST SAYING

Our Children's Births

FIRST CHILD

PHOTOGRAPHS

_____
FULL NAME

_____
NICKNAME

_____
TIME AND DATE OF BIRTH

_____
WEIGHT

_____
PLACE

_____
DOCTOR/MIDWIFE

_____
EXPECTED DUE DATE

_____
WHEREABOUTS OF MOTHER AND FATHER WHEN
LABOR PAINS BEGAN

_____
LENGTH OF LABOR

_____
MOST DISTINGUISHING FEATURE AS A NEWBORN

_____
FIRST VISITORS

SPECIAL EVENTS IN THE NEWS THAT DAY

_____

_____

_____

_____

SECOND CHILD

_____
FULL NAME

_____
NICKNAME

_____
TIME AND DATE OF BIRTH

_____
WEIGHT

_____
PLACE

_____
DOCTOR/MIDWIFE

_____
EXPECTED DUE DATE

_____
WHEREABOUTS OF MOTHER AND FATHER WHEN
LABOR PAINS BEGAN

_____
LENGTH OF LABOR

_____
MOST DISTINGUISHING FEATURE AS A NEWBORN

_____
FIRST VISITORS

SPECIAL EVENTS IN THE NEWS THAT DAY

_____

_____

_____

_____

_____

THIRD CHILD

FULL NAME

NICKNAME

TIME AND DATE OF BIRTH

WEIGHT

PLACE

DOCTOR/MIDWIFE

EXPECTED DUE DATE

WHEREABOUTS OF MOTHER AND FATHER WHEN
LABOR PAINS BEGAN

LENGTH OF LABOR

MOST DISTINGUISHING FEATURE AS A NEWBORN

FIRST VISITORS

SPECIAL EVENTS IN THE NEWS THAT DAY

FOURTH CHILD

FULL NAME

NICKNAME

TIME AND DATE OF BIRTH

WEIGHT

PLACE

DOCTOR/MIDWIFE

EXPECTED DUE DATE

WHEREABOUTS OF MOTHER AND FATHER WHEN
LABOR PAINS BEGAN

LENGTH OF LABOR

MOST DISTINGUISHING FEATURE AS A NEWBORN

FIRST VISITORS

SPECIAL EVENTS IN THE NEWS THAT DAY

Of all the joys that brighten suffering earth, What joy is welcom'd like a newborn child!
CAROLINE NORTON

Our Children as Little Ones

How time flies! For most parents, it seems only yesterday that their confident, strapping
(and often fully grown up!) children were tiny bundles that relied upon their every attention.
What were your children like as little ones?

WHEN DID YOUR BABIES FIRST SLEEP THROUGH THE NIGHT?

_____

_____

WHAT WERE THEIR FIRST WORDS, AND AT WHAT AGE DID THEY BEGIN TO TALK?

_____

_____

WHEN DID THEY BEGIN TO WALK? DESCRIBE ANY MAYHEM THAT ENSUED!

_____

_____

WHEN DID THEY BEGIN TEETHING?

_____

_____

DID THEY HAVE FAVORITE TOYS (OR OBJECTS!) THAT ACCOMPANIED THEM EVERYWHERE?

_____

_____

Photographs

Share any special stories about your children when they were babies and toddlers, be they humorous moments, rascally escapades, or touching events.

_____

_____

_____

_____

_____

_____

_____

_____

_____

_____

Photographs

Babies are such a nice way to start people.
DON HEROLD

Our Home Sweet Home

Your family may have lived in just one house over the years or possibly many. Share the joys of building, renovating, restoring, and expanding; all the hard work that might have gone into making your house a home!

ADDRESS

_____

_____

DESCRIPTION OF HOUSE

_____

PERIOD OF RESIDENCE

_____

MEMORIES

_____

_____

ADDRESS

_____

_____

DESCRIPTION OF HOUSE

_____

PERIOD OF RESIDENCE

_____

MEMORIES

_____

_____

ADDRESS

_____

_____

DESCRIPTION OF HOUSE

_____

PERIOD OF RESIDENCE

_____

MEMORIES

_____

_____

ADDRESS

_____

_____

DESCRIPTION OF HOUSE

_____

PERIOD OF RESIDENCE

_____

MEMORIES

_____

_____

Photographs

Seek home for rest,
For home is best.
THOMAS TUSSER, FIVE HUNDRED POINTS OF GOOD HUSBANDRY

Our Family Vehicles

Quite often, the family car goes hand-in-hand with family adventures (and, sometimes, misadventures – depending on the temperament of the car!). Recall the different cars your family has owned over the years.

OWNER

MAKE/MODEL/YEAR

DURATION OF OWNERSHIP

ANECDOTES

OWNER

MAKE/MODEL/YEAR

DURATION OF OWNERSHIP

ANECDOTES

OWNER

MAKE/MODEL/YEAR

DURATION OF OWNERSHIP

ANECDOTES

OWNER

MAKE/MODEL/YEAR

DURATION OF OWNERSHIP

ANECDOTES

OWNER

MAKE/MODEL/YEAR

DURATION OF OWNERSHIP

ANECDOTES

OWNER

MAKE/MODEL/YEAR

DURATION OF OWNERSHIP

ANECDOTES

Photographs

My life is passing in front of my eyes. The worst part is I'm driving a used car.
WOODY ALLEN, MANHATTAN MURDER MYSTERY

Our Family Holidays

All family holidays – be they spent traveling across country, or basking at a luxurious resort – produce special memories.

LOCATION _____ DATE VISITED _____

SPECIAL MEMORIES

_____

_____

_____

_____

_____

LOCATION _____ DATE VISITED _____

SPECIAL MEMORIES

_____

_____

_____

_____

_____

LOCATION _____ DATE VISITED _____

SPECIAL MEMORIES

_____

_____

_____

_____

Photographs

LOCATION   DATE VISITED

SPECIAL MEMORIES

LOCATION   DATE VISITED

SPECIAL MEMORIES

LOCATION   DATE VISITED

SPECIAL MEMORIES

Photographs

When I am in the country, I wish to vegetate like the country.
WILLIAM HAZLITT

Our Workplaces

Love it (and sometimes hate it!) work is what puts bread and butter on your family's table.
Write down the jobs your family members have held over the years.

NAME

_____

POSITIONS HELD AND DATES

_____

_____

MENTORS/COLORFUL CHARACTERS IN THE WORKPLACE

_____

WHAT DID YOU DREAM OF BECOMING WHEN YOU GREW UP?

_____

CURRENT DREAM JOB

NAME

_____

POSITIONS HELD AND DATES

_____

_____

MENTORS/COLORFUL CHARACTERS IN THE WORKPLACE

_____

WHAT DID YOU DREAM OF BECOMING WHEN YOU GREW UP?

_____

CURRENT DREAM JOB

NAME

_____

POSITIONS HELD AND DATES

_____

_____

MENTORS/COLORFUL CHARACTERS IN THE WORKPLACE

_____

WHAT DID YOU DREAM OF BECOMING WHEN YOU GREW UP?

_____

CURRENT DREAM JOB

NAME

POSITIONS HELD AND DATES

MENTORS/COLORFUL CHARACTERS IN THE WORKPLACE

WHAT DID YOU DREAM OF BECOMING WHEN YOU GREW UP?

CURRENT DREAM JOB

NAME

POSITIONS HELD AND DATES

MENTORS/COLORFUL CHARACTERS IN THE WORKPLACE

WHAT DID YOU DREAM OF BECOMING WHEN YOU GREW UP?

CURRENT DREAM JOB

NAME

POSITIONS HELD AND DATES

MENTORS/COLORFUL CHARACTERS IN THE WORKPLACE

WHAT DID YOU DREAM OF BECOMING WHEN YOU GREW UP?

CURRENT DREAM JOB

Laziness may appear attractive, but work gives satisfaction.
ANNE FRANK

Our School Years

"No more pencils, no more books, no more teachers' dirty looks…" is a rhyme many American children joyously chant at the end of each school term! Share your family's experiences of school.

NAME

PRESCHOOL   DATES OF ATTENDANCE

ELEMENTARY SCHOOL   DATES OF ATTENDANCE

HIGH SCHOOL   DATES OF ATTENDANCE

COLLEGE/UNIVERSITY   DATES OF ATTENDANCE

CERTIFICATES OR DEGREES ACHIEVED

BEST SUBJECTS

WORST SUBJECTS

FAVORITE TEACHERS

BEST FRIENDS AT SCHOOL

HAPPIEST MEMORIES OF SCHOOL

NAME

PRESCHOOL   DATES OF ATTENDANCE

ELEMENTARY SCHOOL   DATES OF ATTENDANCE

HIGH SCHOOL   DATES OF ATTENDANCE

COLLEGE/UNIVERSITY   DATES OF ATTENDANCE

CERTIFICATES OR DEGREES ACHIEVED

BEST SUBJECTS

WORST SUBJECTS

FAVORITE TEACHERS

BEST FRIENDS AT SCHOOL

HAPPIEST MEMORIES OF SCHOOL

NAME

PRESCHOOL   DATES OF ATTENDANCE

ELEMENTARY SCHOOL   DATES OF ATTENDANCE

HIGH SCHOOL   DATES OF ATTENDANCE

COLLEGE/UNIVERSITY   DATES OF ATTENDANCE

CERTIFICATES OR DEGREES ACHIEVED

BEST SUBJECTS

WORST SUBJECTS

FAVORITE TEACHERS

BEST FRIENDS AT SCHOOL

HAPPIEST MEMORIES OF SCHOOL

NAME

PRESCHOOL   DATES OF ATTENDANCE

ELEMENTARY SCHOOL   DATES OF ATTENDANCE

HIGH SCHOOL   DATES OF ATTENDANCE

COLLEGE/UNIVERSITY   DATES OF ATTENDANCE

CERTIFICATES OR DEGREES ACHIEVED

BEST SUBJECTS

WORST SUBJECTS

FAVORITE TEACHERS

BEST FRIENDS AT SCHOOL

HAPPIEST MEMORIES OF SCHOOL

NAME

PRESCHOOL   DATES OF ATTENDANCE

ELEMENTARY SCHOOL   DATES OF ATTENDANCE

HIGH SCHOOL   DATES OF ATTENDANCE

COLLEGE/UNIVERSITY   DATES OF ATTENDANCE

CERTIFICATES OR DEGREES ACHIEVED

BEST SUBJECTS

WORST SUBJECTS

FAVORITE TEACHERS

BEST FRIENDS AT SCHOOL

HAPPIEST MEMORIES OF SCHOOL

NAME

PRESCHOOL   DATES OF ATTENDANCE

ELEMENTARY SCHOOL   DATES OF ATTENDANCE

HIGH SCHOOL   DATES OF ATTENDANCE

COLLEGE/UNIVERSITY   DATES OF ATTENDANCE

CERTIFICATES OR DEGREES ACHIEVED

BEST SUBJECTS

WORST SUBJECTS

FAVORITE TEACHERS

BEST FRIENDS AT SCHOOL

HAPPIEST MEMORIES OF SCHOOL

"Whom are you?" said he, for he had been to night school.
GEORGE ADE

Our Sports and Games

Whether it be serious sporting or just for fun, some families' weekends are a series of taxiing children from playing field to playing field! Then again, you may have a family who love their sports, but choose to indulge whilst firmly planted on the couch!

FAVORITE SPORTS

FAVORITE TEAMS/SPORTS PEOPLE

SPORTS PLAYED

SPORTING ACHIEVEMENTS/ACCOLADES

BACKYARD SPORTS/GAMES

SPORTING ANECDOTES

Photographs

Photographs

Photographs

I'm the greatest golfer. I just have not played yet.
MUHAMMAD ALI

Our Family Pastimes

Some families go fishing, other families enjoy videos and popcorn, while other families again partake in gruelling family 'fun' runs! How does your family like to relax in its spare time?

FAVORITE RECREATIONAL ACTIVITIES

_____

_____

_____

_____

ANECDOTES

_____

_____

_____

_____

Photographs

Photographs

Photographs

Man cannot live by bread alone; he must have peanut butter.
JAMES A. GARFIELD

Our Good Times

Such is life that all families will have their ups and downs.
While we savor the moments of joy and hope that the scales will tip this way for the most part of our lives, unfortunately,
happiness is tempered with moments of sadness and disappointment.

ANECDOTES

_____

_____

_____

_____

_____

_____

_____

_____

_____

_____

Our Bad Times

ANECDOTES

_____

_____

_____

_____

_____

_____

_____

_____

_____

_____

_____

_____

_____

_____

A proverb is no proverb to you till life has illustrated it.

Our Family Pets

Whether it be four-legged, furry, scaled, or feathered, the family pet inevitably becomes a much loved member of the family, well-behaved or not! These creatures sometimes not only share your daily activities, but run them!

NAME _____ TYPE OF PET _____

ADOPTIVE 'PARENT/S' _____

HOW THIS PET CAME INTO OUR LIVES _____

LOVABLE QUALITIES _____ NOT-SO-LOVABLE QUALITIES _____

ANECDOTES _____
_____

NAME _____ TYPE OF PET _____

ADOPTIVE 'PARENT/S' _____

HOW THIS PET CAME INTO OUR LIVES _____

LOVABLE QUALITIES _____ NOT-SO-LOVABLE QUALITIES _____

ANECDOTES _____
_____

NAME _____ TYPE OF PET _____

ADOPTIVE 'PARENT/S' _____

HOW THIS PET CAME INTO OUR LIVES _____

LOVABLE QUALITIES _____ NOT-SO-LOVABLE QUALITIES _____

ANECDOTES _____

Photographs

Animals are such agreeable friends – they ask no questions, they pass no criticisms.
GEORGE ELIOT

Our Family Friends

Most families have friends who virtually become a member of the family, and share in its joys and sorrows.

NAME/S
_____

HOW WE MET
_____

ADMIRABLE QUALITIES
_____

GOOD TIMES WE'VE SHARED
_____

ANECDOTES
_____
_____

NAME/S
_____

HOW WE MET
_____

ADMIRABLE QUALITIES
_____

GOOD TIMES WE'VE SHARED
_____

ANECDOTES
_____
_____

NAME/S
_____

HOW WE MET
_____

ADMIRABLE QUALITIES
_____

GOOD TIMES WE'VE SHARED
_____

ANECDOTES
_____

Photographs

Fate chooses your relations, you choose your friends.
Jacques Delille

Our Family Traditions

Family traditions are often as unique as families themselves!
What traditions do your family keep up?
How did these habits originate and develop over time?

FAMILY TRADITIONS FROM THE FATHER'S SIDE

_____

_____

_____

_____

FAMILY TRADITIONS FROM THE MOTHER'S SIDE

_____

_____

_____

_____

FAMILY TRADITIONS THAT BEGAN WITH OUR OWN FAMILY

_____

_____

_____

_____

Photographs

Such as we are made of, such as we be.
SHAKESPEARE

Our Family Recipes

From traditional recipes passed down from generation to generation, to the inspired pasta put together by a budding young chef, every family has favorite recipes.

RECIPE

ORIGINS

INGREDIENTS

METHOD

RECIPE

ORIGINS

INGREDIENTS

METHOD

RECIPE

ORIGINS

INGREDIENTS

METHOD

RECIPE

ORIGINS

INGREDIENTS

METHOD

RECIPE

ORIGINS

INGREDIENTS

METHOD

RECIPE

ORIGINS

INGREDIENTS

METHOD

RECIPE

ORIGINS

INGREDIENTS

METHOD

RECIPE

ORIGINS

INGREDIENTS

METHOD

Strange to see how a good dinner and feasting reconciles everybody.
SAMUEL PEPYS

Our Special Occasions

There will always be special events which require a family celebration, be they birthdays, anniversaries, or reunions. Share any special stories you have of these occasions – including the venue, why it was held and who was there – and help recall the highs and lows of the event.

Photographs

Our Special Occasions

Photographs

Treasure your families – the future of humanity passes by way of the family.
JOHN PAUL II

Our Special Places

Most families have special places that they like to claim as their own. These places could be anywhere for any number of reasons! Perhaps your family's special place is a spiritual place of worship. But then again, it could be a favorite playground, a ritzy restaurant, or a well-worn picnic spot!

LOCATION

WHY THIS PLACE IS SPECIAL TO US AS A FAMILY

ANECDOTES

LOCATION

WHY THIS PLACE IS SPECIAL TO US AS A FAMILY

ANECDOTES

LOCATION

WHY THIS PLACE IS SPECIAL TO US AS A FAMILY

ANECDOTES

Photographs

Adventure is worthwhile in itself.
AMELIA EARHART

Our Colorful Characters

There is a colorful character or two swinging off most family trees. Sometimes these characters are known as storytellers, adventurers, eccentrics, and, in lesser moments, plain old ratbags!
Record the famous or infamous tales that have made these individuals fall into your family's legend.

NAME

SPECIAL MEMORIES

NAME

SPECIAL MEMORIES

NAME

SPECIAL MEMORIES

NAME

SPECIAL MEMORIES

Photographs

It is indeed desirable to be well descended, but the glory belongs to our ancestors.
PLUTARCH

Our Storytellers

Each family has a storyteller or two who can fill the gaps and recall experiences which color our family history. These stories — be they a triumph against adversity or tales of bravery, kindness, and outstanding achievement — risk being lost forever unless they are written down. Catch up with the storytellers in your family and convert oral history into a written account for all to enjoy.

To forget one's ancestors is to be a brook without source, a tree without root.
Chinese proverb

Our Hopes for the Future

Share your hopes for the future, be they big or small, wildly extravagant, or just within your immediate grasp!

NAME

HOPES FOR THE FUTURE

DATE

NAME

HOPES FOR THE FUTURE

DATE

NAME

HOPES FOR THE FUTURE

DATE

NAME

HOPES FOR THE FUTURE

DATE

NAME

HOPES FOR THE FUTURE

DATE

NAME

HOPES FOR THE FUTURE

DATE

One generation plants the trees; another gets the shade.
CHINESE PROVERB

Our Medical Records

NAME
_____

BLOOD TYPE
_____

ALLERGIES
_____
_____
_____

IMMUNIZATIONS (AND DATES)
_____
_____
_____

SERIOUS ILLNESSES/MEDICAL CONDITIONS
_____
_____

OPERATIONS
_____
_____
_____

NAME
_____

BLOOD TYPE
_____

ALLERGIES
_____
_____
_____

IMMUNIZATIONS (AND DATES)
_____
_____
_____

SERIOUS ILLNESSES/MEDICAL CONDITIONS
_____
_____

OPERATIONS
_____
_____

NAME
_____

BLOOD TYPE
_____

ALLERGIES
_____
_____
_____

IMMUNIZATIONS (AND DATES)
_____
_____
_____

SERIOUS ILLNESSES/MEDICAL CONDITIONS
_____
_____

OPERATIONS
_____
_____

NAME
_____

BLOOD TYPE
_____

ALLERGIES
_____
_____
_____

IMMUNIZATIONS (AND DATES)
_____
_____
_____

SERIOUS ILLNESSES/MEDICAL CONDITIONS
_____
_____

OPERATIONS
_____
_____

Notes

NAME _____

BLOOD TYPE _____

ALLERGIES _____

_____

_____

IMMUNIZATIONS (AND DATES) _____

_____

SERIOUS ILLNESSES/MEDICAL CONDITIONS _____

_____

OPERATIONS _____

_____

NAME _____

BLOOD TYPE _____

ALLERGIES _____

_____

_____

IMMUNIZATIONS (AND DATES) _____

_____

SERIOUS ILLNESSES/MEDICAL CONDITIONS _____

_____

OPERATIONS _____

_____

HISTORY OF SERIOUS ILLNESS/MEDICAL CONDITIONS IN THE EXTENDED FAMILY

_____

_____

_____

_____

_____

_____

_____

_____

I find the medicine worse than the malady.
JOHN FLETCHER, *THE LOVER'S PROGRESS*